SILENCE HAS A NAME

poems by

Arya F. Jenkins

Finishing Line Press
Georgetown, Kentucky

SILENCE HAS A NAME

ACKNOWLEDGMENTS

These poems were initially published in the following journals and magazines:

"Final Words for My Brother," *Dirty Chai* magazine, Issue Two, Winter 2014
"Incorrigible," *Agave Magazine*, June, 2014
"Sleeping Next to Death," *Blue Heron Review*, Winter 2015
"Ode to Green," *Blue Heron Review*, Summer 2015

Editor: Christen Kincaid

Cover Art: Arya F. Jenkins

Author Photo: Arya F. Jenkins

Cover Design: Elizabeth Maines

Printed in the USA on acid-free paper.
Order online: www.finishinglinepress.com
            also available on amazon.com

Author inquiries and mail orders:
Finishing Line Press
P. O. Box 1626
Georgetown, Kentucky 40324
U. S. A.

Table of Contents

"The pain, or the memory of pain, that here was literally sucked away by something nameless until only a void was left. The knowledge that this question was possible: pain that turns finally into emptiness. The knowledge that the same equation applied to everything, more or less."

—Roberto Bolaño, *2666*

INCORRIGIBLE

A single syllable
One word
Escapes
Abandons her constellation
Commits to flight

You hear her
Bursting ramparts
This creature
Departing
Across darkness
Unattended
Incorrigible thing
Warbling madness.

NOTES ON A POET

His mesmerizing words
Are not quite true
Neither is his rumpled façade
Quite humble

Like a false lover
His language is divine
But contrived
Not imagined—

Stolen from the draft of other lives
Escaped narratives

Lies stolen
Analyzed
Packaged and proffered—
As if naturally conceived

You might opine—
Isn't this the task of every poet?
But I disagree!

In order to husk the fruit
You must transgress the wind
Roll back the storm and
Stare straight at the sun
Without illusions
Unflinching

There you will find
Your own raw stones of truth.

FOR MY GREAT GRANDMOTHER
SINGING IN A WINDOWLESS ATTIC

Wordless singsong
Meaningless and full of meaning
Follows me through the years
Calling me back to the beginning
Where she sings still
In an attic full of tears
Imprisoned by a jealous husband

Singing alone
Upstairs
Close to the moon
The imaginary sister
Close to the imaginary sun
My great grandmother died
Mad in her high angled coffin at 29

Her voice unleashed
She whispers still through the trees
Screaming in the eaves
of an eternal night.

SURELY

Surely we grasp at
straws together
all of us, women
refusing to
march to our own drum

Divinely
clasping the tendrils of
never even as we disappear into
work, marriage
whatever will tether us away from
who we are
what we want

Surely some of us
march in defiant dreams and
when somnolent on beaches
behold wars within

Surely the truth
climbs out
in spite of us—

       My mother misplaced
       her glasses in the refrigerator

After years spent in irrelevant occupation
inocular gestation
I come only to this

Victorious emptiness.

ODE TO GREEN

All this so green
All around me
Brimming with possibilities
Even as the fall sets in
And the dust of leaves
Begins to form on the ground

I want my eyes to contain
Everything exactly as it is
So green
Green as it is new
Green as it was
When I was a teenager
Living in Connecticut
A child climbing hills
Outside of Bogota
A child in the garden of Talara, Peru

Green cycles through my memory
I retrieve and press it to my heart
Like a page on which
Are the evanescent names
Of all I have loved
The signifiers—
Green bugs
Long blades of grass
The green inkwell of everything—

Everything as it is now
And was.

NIGHT FULL OF STARS

In the arrangement
Consorts offer each other
To the stars
And the stars in turn
Awaken their milk
Which leaks black
Over their impulses

Their impulses
Interweave arms and legs
And their eyes become
Holes in an abyss
And mouths
The children of myths

Their hearts bleat out
Unholy stories

Only the night remembers
Only the quiet
Writes down.

SLEEPING NEXT TO DEATH

I sleep little
Next to the one who is dying

Couched in my own conceits
Irretrievable in faraway places

While her eyes dim and flutter
Practicing closing for all time

Her hands
Languorous and disconsolate
Rest across her belly

Preparing

And I am her night
Bringing darkness to feed her
Like seeds to a bird in its cage

No matter what I say
Or fail to say
The dark truth between us
Is that she will go
While I will stay

The muses of unrelinquishable loss and grief
Sing this in the space between us.

KEEPING VIGIL

Here she is up close
I try to reach her
But her eyes skitter
Don't want to find me
Too solid and present

She jumps when I approach—
"Too much energy?"
I ask the obvious
She nods

I've been sent way before
By the dying
Who sense
Beyond my calm exterior
The percolating fever
The variegated impulse
Still fulminating

I take the bony hands
The flinching smile
Compressing them into my own
My own eyes closing
My own smile giving way
To the inevitable
Knowing.

FINAL WORDS FOR MY BROTHER

I wasn't there in the hospital with you that last time
Watching tubes leak what they could into your arms
Out of bags half-filled with brine half-filled with time
As our father was there
Wondering how this could be

I wasn't there when your eyes closed
Eyelashes stilled

You might have dreamed of mountains
Rivers, evergreens
Becoming one with them
As they became mere figments
Diminishing in space
Disconnecting you from the past
And the earth you were leaving

So many years and miles away
I felt a joyful reprise in my heart
Your final promise to stop drinking
As if the demon had been unbidden all along
Something apart from you

You promise?
You promise?
I asked that source in me still beating
You promise?

I had wished an end to it so long
Been deceived so often
And still I believed
Even as I closed my eyes
This would be the end of it
No more lies
Only hope now
Instead of death knocking.

MY PARENTS IN THE END

My parents both sang in the end
My mother wrote
My father accomplished crossword puzzles
Putting a pretend trumpet to his mouth
The night he died
While his children danced around him

My mother worked on a short story
Typing on her lap top
Blissful under the influence of morphine
But clear as glass
Just days before she died

The bell tolled and death
Took them both
Their minds sharp as knives
Pinned to the present and past
Even as wind blew out their lungs.

LYRICAL OBEISANCE

To you I bow master note
Master language in whose
Disciplined hands
Salvation offers all
A second chance

Bebop I dry my eyes
Bebop I blow the blues
Bebop I allay my soul's
Confusion in this tremor of notes
Lyrical assuaging hope

Let there be no interference to the song
Let it blow and blow
Uninterrupted through time
A line of musical invention
Rising in counterpoint to the sun.

REACHING

We make arrangements because we are not divine. Lighting one another's cigarettes, we sit on a stoop, listen to jazz, voices breaking in between all the stillness and static vying for attention. We attend only to our whispers and the smoke rising out of everything: the air, the sea, the clouds, vehicles passing by, and of course ourselves.

And always this wondering, even as I reach for you, always, how long we will be here speaking, or trying to speak, the smoke between us. How long it will be until we disperse too.

TELL MEMORY

I don't ask anything of memory
Except that it remain in its place
Hidden among the leaves
The eaves of the past in which
Only ghosts and cobwebs reside—

I am not a spider and have
No desire to crawl in the
Attic with her anymore

Let her holler unattended
Spoiled child that she is
Let her beg to be brought down to
Dinner and served with the adults

She will spoil our meal, I tell you
Her accusing glances will
Spark talk and from there
Anything is possible

Tell memory I want
No part of her anymore
She has done enough damage
Rearranging my things
Creating divisions in my family
Calling out those long gone
As if they could still do justice to
Failed circumstances

Tell her to go now
To find youth elsewhere
Springing among the greens of
Other remembrances
Other pasts
But not my own

For I am done with her.

NOW THAT I AM HERE

Now that I am less tired
And refuse to sleep
Now that I prefer to listen to truth
Rather than to lies
Now that I am here
Attending to silence
Instead of rumors

There is no going back—
Only the sky
And the unutterably beautiful landscape
Mother-shaped
And stretched out
Long as time
Begging us to forgive her.

IMPERMANENCE

Nothing has changed. We attend to the same questions, get up with the same doubts. Lately, standing after sitting a long time in meditation, I uncramp, feeling time. My bones ache from caffeine, I tell myself, nothing more. Even as memories impel my mind along with lists of what I must do—my father and mother and their sins done, now gone; all the people I have known, moved on. I too wait for spring, even as I gather myself like something unfurling and turning within, afraid to lose itself and gathering all it knows for safekeeping somewhere.

The momentum of spring with its dust of anticipation seizes my ankles and breaks my heart that is tender from so much leaving.

Could I promise myself not to go? Could I keep that promise in spite of everything? No, I tell myself, I know now I can't. For all is impermanence, even this hope and love.

ODE TO THE RAINBOW

Beyond the obstacles and intemperance
The silence and regret
Beyond the terror of
Death herself circumcising
Colors arise in transcendent flavor
Tagging the absolving sky.

Arya F. Jenkins's poetry, fiction and creative nonfiction have appeared in journals such as *Agave Magazine, Brilliant Corners, Burrow Press Review, Cleaver Magazine, The Feminist Wire* and *Provincetown Arts Magazine*. Her poetry was nominated for a Pushcart Prize in 2015, and her poetry and essays have been included in three anthologies. She writes short stories for *Jerry Jazz Musician*, which commissioned her to write jazz fiction. Her poetry chapbook, *JEWEL FIRE*, was published by AllBook Books.